# Book Of Poems

A book of poetry on everything I love to appreciate

Abdiel Raphael Fenn

BookLeaf Publishing

India | USA | UK

Made with ❤ on the BookLeaf Publishing Platform

www.bookleafpub.in

www.bookleafpub.com

# Dedication

## *To My God, to Parents And Grandparents.*

I would like to thank my God , my parents and grandparents who helped me embark on this poem writing journey and realising my interest in creating poems. I am thankful for their inputs in this creation and acknowledge that I wouldn't have been able to compete the challenge without their support .

# Preface

I have always loved listening to poems when I was small.When I was 9,I decided to make a book of poems.I faced many challenges like not having time to write.I also had to go to school and do homework.But,I overcame these challenges and made this book.I'm sure you'll love it!

# Acknowledgements

I thank my Lord and saviour
Jesus Christ,
my parents and my grandparents.

**What a fine day it is to look at the wide sky,**
**the Sun shining bright.**
In the morning, it is so cool,
I'd be happy to jump right into the pool!
**It is so fun to run,**
**While getting vitamin D from the sun!**
When you get up from bed
you will feel refreshed.
When you go to school,
you can see the dew.
When you see the sky,
It is a true delight!

# 2. A Sunny Morning

**What a fine day it is to look at the wide sky,**
**the Sun shining bright.**
In the morning, it is so cool,
I'd be happy to jump right into the pool!
**It is so fun to run,**
**While getting vitamin D from the sun!**
When you get up from bed
you will feel refreshed.
When you go to school,
you can see the dew.
When you see the sky,
It is a true delight!

# 3. Our Universe

There is something about our universe which makes it
unique,
Aren't the Sun and stars just magnifique!
When we look into the sky, the planets, galaxies,
It makes one wonder who made these.
Some astronauts went to space
And are having such a struggle to come back.
I wanted to be an astronaut,
But now I wonder, I am taken aback.
Mercury or Mars, Saturn or Jupiter,
Some have moons, some have none,
What is this awesomeness yonder, I often wonder.
When I go to sleep tonight,
In my dreams, I should take a flight,
and explore it's every hidden mystery,
and come back to Earth and write its' story.

# 4. Teamwork

Teamwork makes the dream work,
One may work hard,
one may work fast,
but when one works in a group,
there are inputs from a whole troop.
A team is unity,
a team is strength,
a team is about love, selflessness and help.
When all the members of the team strive for victory,
the competitors must be careful because they are in
jeopardy!

# 5. Sleep

Precious sleep

To sleep is important,
To sleep is essential,
It is part of our circadian rhythm,
which should not be thought trivial.

Animals also sleep
Birds also sleep
Its just the way they keep healthy,
After a full day of work,
Thats the way to become wealthy.

Look at humans,
The animals seem to know better,
We play, we work all day long,
When we should sleep,
We browse our phones and scroll,
And let our night sleep and dreams take a stroll
And lose out on our goal.
When we learn from people who have time and again
said
Not wealth, but food, family and sleep
Are the ones we must keep
And not act as one without self control...put down that
phone!

# 6. Cancer is troublesome

Cancer
Cancer is such a bother
Suspect it when you least expect it
If you forget, it will collect
Your dignity, your money, your neck
Carcinoma breast, take a test
It happens mostly to women, in the prime of their health
Though they may be young or old
The disease must be controlled
Carcinoma lung, it sucks your breath
And sends you to your death
Stop smoking
If you want to avoid a choking.

# 7. Failures are the stepping stones

Oh how I wish
I would win an award
for everything i participate in..
Reality couldn't be more far fetched
It has made me so poetic
Oh the sorrow, oh the pain,
Everytime I fail
Every time they fail to recognize my talent, my skill
I feel so disheartened
My heart so burdened
It feels like it is lost
There is always such a cost
to pay, in pain..

But, be not disheartened, Oh dear heart
We can always have a fresh start
The world was not fashioned in a day
We must learn to wait,
If Thomas Edison had given up
just for a mere 1000 failures,
We would be in the dark at night
Waiting eagerly for sunlight
I will ,therefore, yet try,
I will yet wait,
I will keep on working hard,
Running on and on,
till I see the glimpse of victory,
that has been hiding ahead of me, then failure will be a
mere shadow , that powerlessly fades away.

# 8. Seashore

Let the seashore make your day,
Let it take your sorrows and pains away,
Have you been to the beach today,
To watch the waves rise and sway.

How vast is the seashore,
Where does it begin and where does it end,
Can anyone count the numerous grains of sand,
Does anyone know from where it all came.

I collect sea shells on the seashore,
These were brought by the ocean waves,
I see tiny crabs running around,
Hiding in their burrow when chased,
Mother, when will you take me to the seashore again?
When can i bring my sand toys to play?

# 9. Hope

Hope is such a positive thing,
Never leave it out of your daily living,
In every situation, good or bad,
In every situation, happy or sad,
Bring a bag full of hope for the day
It will carry you through the journey, I must say.

Hope deferred makes the heart sick
Without hope, there is no kick
Those who hope do not fall sick
Hope in something, it will make you stick.

Where there is hope, there is life
There is unending joy and no more strife
If you have in noone or nothing to hope,
Hope in God, your Creator and you will have scope.

# 10. Fruits and vegetables

Fruits and vegetables,
They are so healthy,
Fill your plates full of them,
Because they are so very worthy.
An apple a day keeps a doctor away,
VIBGYOR, fill your plates with colourful fruits, they say,
Vitamins and minerals, water and fibre,
How beneficial they are, there is no describer,
75 percent of our plate, should constitute fruits and
veggies,
Then you won't fall sick,
You'll always be healthy.
My mother has a way to make me eat them,
It should not be a struggle,
Fruit custard, milkshakes, desserts and juices and
puddings,
They are so yummy and amazing.

# 11. Books- a beacon of knowledge

Books are a vast ocean of knowledge,
you must read a few pages everyday,
To increase your knowledge, skill and passion,
To never run out of fashion.

Books have many benefits,
Can you think of few,
They also make us calm,
They teach us focus and concentration,
And patience and motivation.
It increases your vocabulary and exercises your brain,
Before you realize it,
you have developed excellent memory.

So, take a time to read some book every day,
In this evil age we live in,
It will keep our mental health at bay.

Read a book for good sleep,
Gift a book to a friend today,
Realize that people may come and go,
But a book is a friend who will stay.

# 12. Our God

Our God is a kind and loving God,
Quick to forgive,
Quick to show mercy ,
To the truly repentant heart.

There is no sin He doesn't forgive,
There is no human he doesn't love,
He is our very present help in times of trouble,
We can always run up to Him.

He is a very righteous judge,
He may excuse for a while,
He will pronounce judgement one day,
Make sure you don't get carried away.

Kiss His feet lest He be angry with you,
Love Him is what He wants from you
One day should not pass by
Without you talking to your Father Heavenly
Who waits affectionately for you and constantly...

# 13. Friendship is a gift

Friendship

Friendship is something that cannot be destroyed,
Even though your friends can make you annoyed,
Friendship is showing someone that they are not alone,
You are showing friendship even when you are calling
them on phone,
You meet friends at home or school,
You can also have a party in a pool,
Friendship is something that cannot be broken,
Friendship is as tasty as French toast and cinnamon..

# 14. Rainbows are poetic

Rainbows

Rainbows are things we knew since we were toddlers,
They are amazing,
They consists of endless colours,
When I look at the rainbow,
It makes me relaxed when I am sitting,
They may have light colours,
Which are used to colour flowers,
Finally, rainbows are something that EMIT joy,
I go out and admire them with my friend Roy.

Rainbow are created when sun is reflected through
water,
Rainbows are created when light passes through the
prism,
Rainbows are bow shaped, they look like a canopy,
The very sight of it makes everyone happy.
Rainbow is mentioned in the Bible in Noah's story,
If you want to read about it, go and see,
It was a covenant between God and he.

# 15. Cold

The common cold
Have you ever been affected by the common cold,
It is one of the worst things that one can hold,
It makes you so sick that you start to feel old,
Noses pouring, noses sneezing, noses stuffy,
It sure knows how to make your life crappy,

Is there really any treatment for cold,
Whenever the doctor prescribes medicines it doesn't
seem to work,
Symptoms seem to persist,
No matter the hard work.

When I get a cold
I can't seem to do anything much,
Merely lying down and sleeping,
Is the only thing I can touch.
When three days pass by,
It seems to subside on its own,
All my efforts to make it go were unknown,
Have you tried steam,
Have you tried saline,
These are the only things
That bring you back align.

Of all the diseases in the world,
The common cold seems so simple,
How can such troublesome symptoms,
Come out of something so humble..

# 16. Teddy bear

Stuffed animals
I have so many stuffies at home,
I have collected them over a long period of time,
Black, brown, rainbow or yellow,
Such a beautiful collection I have, so mellow.
These stuffed animals may look simple,
But when I look at them I see in them a friend,
To hold them in my hand is so warm and cute,
Having them around fills me with gratitude.
I am thankful for my parents who got them for me,
Whenever I feel alone,
I just like to touch them and hug them,
They seem to emanate so much love,
But when I speak to them,
Why don't they reply.
I take them to travel, take them to sleep,
They all have a name, that's why I must keep
When kids come to my home they all want to take one,
But I can't let take, they are all so special to me,
If we love people like we love stuffies,
This world would be a happier place to be.

# 17. Flood

Floods
Water, water everywhere ,
Cars and people are down under ,
What can we do to avoid the snare ,
And make sure that it never thunders.

We must plant more trees,
So that we do not appease
These waters who love destruction,
And would snuff away all our   construction .

We must build more reservoirs,
Or we will be writing our own memoirs,
Be careful when there are floods,
The seemingly harmless waters,
Stay at home I say,
Lest you want to be carried away.

Practice responsible human behaviour always,
Floods are not always natural disasters,
Off late they are also man made,
Don't destroy the environment too much,
Or else you will find yourself caught in the nature's
clutch.

# 18. Appliances

Fridge and air conditioner
Fridge and ac are two complex appliances,
That have frozen nitrogen as their alliance,
One is used for storing food and drink,
And the other keeps us from becoming pink,
Fridge is also called a refrigerator,
It uses lot less power,
It works for years without a problem,
A stabilizer is not needed for its function solemn,

And ac is also called air conditioner,
It makes hot air disappear and become unpopular,
It lasts for 5 years without a problem,
After which it becomes a complex conundrum.

# 19. Perseverance is the key

Perseverance

Have you ever heard of perseverance,
It is something worth observance,
It is the sister of patience,
It doesn't give up in any circumstance.

They say perseverance is the key,
One has to work hard to succeed,
But hard work is not always the key,
Putting in effort, consistency and not giving up, it's
needed, I agree
He who constantly works towards his goal,
Not giving up,
Constantly sowing his seed,
This is only called perseverance,
The secret to succeed.

There maybe failures, there may be fears,
All sorts of hindrances can come your way,
But if you have the mind to persevere,
Your hands and feet won't sway.

Now you know why we should persevere,
Tell that to your discouraged friend so that they can
hear,
Support is always there,
If you have the mind to find it,
You will find the people who care,
With your team, you must constantly persevere,
You can then taste success with your near and dear.

# 20. Honourable parents

Our parents

Our parents have been our companions from childhood,
They have given birth to us,
They have been our nurturers,
They have encouraged us,
And done everything for us.
Parents are lovely,
Parents are kind,
Tell me if truly you can find anyone,
With such beautiful mind.
They share their everything,
They hold nothing behind,
They always want to see you happy, fulfilled and kind.
In this world that we live in,
We find many friends, good and bad,
But of all, parents are the only ones,
We can be always sure,
Genuinely have our best interest at hand.
No one loves like a parent,
Parents are a gift from God,
Our only prayer must be always,
To be worthy children of theirs,
And reciprocate and return their love,
If only there were ways to do that,
To show the same surplus love,
Selfless, kind and caring,
To the ones who always think of us in their hearts in a
way unending!

# 21. Lovely teachers

My teachers

When we are kids, we go to school,
We have teachers there,
Who teach us and rule,
Who agrees with me,
Teachers can be quiet scary.
I don't know what can make them angry,
But most of them are quite lovely.

When I think of a teacher's heart,
How genuine they are,
They decided to teach,
They had the heart to share their knowledge,
They had the hard to impart courage,
Not everyone can have a heart to teach,
Teachers are light, teachers are guides,
They are the ones we spend most of our time with ,
cannot avoid.
They are our parents in school,
Can you imagine how life would be without them, not
very cool.
They have a big role in shaping and moulding our lives,
Do we see all the hard work and love in their eyes.
Loving teacher's influence goes a long way,
Such teacher's student will never go astray.
A teachers profession is the most noble,
To be able to mould children's future into something
good is most desirable.